Bound for Botany Bay

The First Fleet & the Convict Years

The hulks and the jails had some thousands in store,
But out of the jails are ten thousands more,
Who live by fraud, cheating, vile tricks and foul play,
And should all be sent over to Botany Bay.

TRADITIONAL SONG, 1790

GEOFF HOCKING

Contents

THE LONDON CONVICT MAID.

But sin my youthful heart betrayed,
And now I am a Convict Maid.

To wed my lover I did try,
To take my master's property,
So all my guilt was soon displayed,
And I became a Convict Maid.

Then I was soon to prison sent,
To wait in fear my punishment,
When at the bar I stood dismayed,
Since doomed to be a Convict Maid.

At length the Judge did me address,
Which filled
To Botany B
For seven yea

For seven yea
While my poor
My lover wept, and thus he said,
May God be with my Convict Maid.

To you that hear my mournful tale

Charlotte W——, the subject of this narrative, is a native of London, born of honest parents, she was early taught the value and importance of honesty and virtue; but unhapily ere her attaining the age of maturity, her youthful affections were placed on a young Tradesman, and to raise money to marry her lover, she yielded to the temptation to rob her master, and his property being found in her possession, she was immediately ap-

29 April 1770

SEVENTEEN YEARS HAD PASSED since Captain James Cook had planted the Queen Anne flag of Great Britain on Australia's eastern shore. The British Government was keen that an Englishman should be the 'discoverer' of the unclaimed land mass that the rest of the world was certain lay somewhere out there in the almost uncharted southern hemisphere.

The unknown land was dubbed *'terra incognita'* and although Dutch, Portuguese and French ships had been bumping into the western shoreline for centuries, nobody had ever bothered to take possession. It may be that the shoreline looked uninviting — there were no coastal towns, no bustling ports, no buildings, forts or streets: nothing to invade and therefore nothing to possess.

Cook noted that the natives he encountered when he stepped ashore in 1770 wanted nothing at all, except maybe some of the food he offered them. He also noted that the natives seemed to own nothing themselves, so the land was declared to be *'terra nullius'* [land belonging to no one] and the British made plans to move in. In 1788, the first boatloads of British arrived at Botany Bay to take up permanent residence.

These 'first Australians' arrived in chains.

The Prison Hulks

DUE TO OVERFLOWING PRISONS in Britain, the British Government used a huge **flotilla** of obsolete warships as floating prisons.

These rotting hulks did not improve the beauty of the English seaside ports, and the stench that came from the poor wretches imprisoned on the hulks for years on end caused the authorities to seek a better place for society's human refuse.

Australia seemed just the right place, and it was from these prison ships that the **convicts** of the First Fleet were taken to Botany Bay.

(above)
Portsmouth Harbour with Prison Hulks
Rex Nan Kivell Collection NK815, National Library of Australia, an227394-1

(left)
Captain Arthur Phillip
National Library of Australia Collection, an9846228

Captain Arthur Phillip R.N.

13 May 1787

UNDER THE COMMAND of Captain Arthur Phillip R.N. the First Fleet of 11 ships carrying 717 convicts, 191 marines and 19 officers set sail from Portsmouth, England on 13 May 1787, bound for the newly discovered continent of Australia.

Forty of these people of the First Fleet died on the voyage. However, when the fleet lay at anchor just off the coast of New South Wales on 20 January 1788, they were carrying two more passengers than when they had departed. Forty-two babies were born on board, there being 170 female convicts amongst the transported prisoners.

20 January 1788

CAPTAIN PHILLIP was not all that impressed with Botany Bay, so he took a long-boat and sailed a little further up the coast until he discovered a bay he described as 'the finest harbour in the world, in which a thousand ships of the line may ride in the most perfect security'. He had sailed into Port Jackson (Sydney Harbour) and returned to his ship the *Supply* and prepared to bring the fleet back to this safe harbour.

26 January 1788

On HIS RETURN TO BOTANY BAY, Phillip discovered two French ships lying out to sea, unable to come closer to shore due to unfavourable winds. Phillip rushed back to his harbour the following day and raised the British flag to stake his claim for the **British Crown** in Australia, and beat the French to this glorious prize.

While the British were the first to raise a national flag on Australia's shores, they were also the first to build their prisons on the shoreline of the prettiest bay in the world.

Australia Day

While 26 January is celebrated as the birthday of the Australian nation, it was hardly any cause for celebration for those poor wretches who had spent eight months chained together below decks on the transport ships.

When they were landed, there was no shelter, no settlement, no roads, and no food supplies except for what they had brought with them. For most convicts it seemed as if there was no hope for them at all.

To make matters worse, they spent the next few months building their own prisons, and attempting to clear some land, till the soil and sow their own food.

As very few knew anything at all about farming or building, it is hardly surprising that in the first year they nearly starved, until the Second Fleet arrived with fresh supplies.

Convicts of New Holland
Dixson Galleries, State Library of New South Wales

EYED SUE, and SWEET POLL of PLYMOUTH,
e leave of their Lovers who are going to Botany Bay.

Bound for Botany Bay

This is the best known of all the convict laments. However, it was not a song written at the time of transportation but much later, in the 1850s, by the goldfields minstrel, Charles Thatcher.

Farewell to old England for ever,
Farewell to my rum culls as well;
Farewell to the well-known Old Bailee,
Where I used to cut such a swell.

Singing too-ral li-ooral li-ad-dity
Singing too-ral li-ooral li-ay;
Singing too-ral li-ooral li-ad-dity
And we're bound for Botany Bay.

There's the captain as is our commander,
There's the bo'sun and all the ship's crew,
There's the first and second-class passengers,
Knows what we poor convicts go through.

'Taint leavin' old England we cares about,
'Taint cos we mispels what we knows,
But becos all we light-fingered gentry
Hops around with a log on our toes.

For seven long years I'll be staying there,
For seven long years and a day,
For meeting a cove in an area
And taking his ticker away.

Oh, had I the wings of a turtle-dove!
I'd soar on my pinions so high,
Slap bang to the arms of my Polly love,
And in her sweet presence I'd die.

Now, all my young Dookies and Duchesses,
Take warning from what I've to say,
Mind all is your own as you touchesses,
Or you'll find us in Botany Bay.

Unfit for Work

The Governor of Van Diemen's Land George Arthur wrote to the Minister for the **Colonies** in England and complained that: 'the quality of the convicts assigned as agricultural labourers was poor and inappropriate — doddering octogenarians; weak, half-imbecile boys; Cockney barbers; professional thieves whose hard labour had been lifting purses and breaking locks — men who could not, or would not, work, and took every opportunity to destroy the tools and other property of masters who tried to make them do so'.

Of course Australia was marked for glory, for its people had been chosen by the finest judges in England.

A Hazardous Journey

THE VOYAGE aboard a convict transport was no sea-cruise. The convicts were chained together below decks for weeks on end, their rations were meagre to say the least, and the stench as they lay amongst their own filth was unbelievable.

Almost one-quarter of all who embarked from England's shores never reached their destination, hundreds perished at sea and their naked bodies were cast over the side, their clothes having been taken from them as soon as the last breath passed from their lips.

The chaplain of New South Wales on entering one of the ships was turned back by the stench coming from the hold. He saw half of those within lying semi-naked without beds or bedding, almost unable to move themselves about.

Several convicts died when they were brought up on deck, their bodies simply thrown over the side and left naked on the rocks where the waves had tossed them.

Once on shore, the convicts were housed in tents and had to lie on the bare ground with only one blanket to cover four of them. Their heads and clothes were filthy and infested with lice, they suffered from scurvy, and were violently ill, howling and wailing all night long.

Adieu, Adieu My Native Land, Allport Library and Museum of Fine Arts, State Library of Tasmania.

Convicts Embarking for Botany Bay
Rex Nan Kivell Collection NK228, National Library of Australia, an5601547

An Ugly Warning

In the 18th century, bodies were left hanging from **gibbet posts** all along the English coastline as a constant reminder of the harsh penalties paid out to those who dared to break the Queen's laws.

It seemed to have little or no effect at all. The courts were never without cases to hear and the prison hulks were never emptied, no matter how many convicts were transported to the colonies.

9

Hard Labour and the Lash

ONCE THE CONVICTS were landed off the transport ships they were put to work. Few of the girls could milk a cow, make butter or sew a stitch, or even scrub a floor. Most were street-walkers who spent their days and their nights hanging about tavern doors, going with any man who could stand them the price of a pint of gin.

The men were put to work breaking rocks in the quarries or on the roads. While convict labour built much of the **infrastructure** of old Sydney Town that survives into the present day, few convicts ever benefitted from their labours, hundreds died with the steel ball still shackled to their ankles.

One convict recalled the brutal treatment by the overseers and the punishment given to those who dared defy the law:

'We have to work from 14 to 18 hours a day, sometimes up to our knees in cold water, 'til we are ready to sink with fatigue. After four of us had refused to go to work the inhuman driver struck one with a heavy thong, which caused the gang to rise and dreadfully beat the drivers, by which one died the same day.

'The soldiers were immediately sent for, and 47 of us immediately taken into custody. Nine were sentenced to die, and 18 were sentenced to go to the mercury mines to work underground. On Saturday we were all paraded in front of the scaffold. The nine unfortunate men came on with a firm step, the chaplain taking leave of them. The **executioner** commenced tying them up to the beam, by which they hang 16 at a time. The nine men seemed to cry out with one voice, "We die happy!".'

They preferred a quick death to a slow one of beatings and brutality on the chain gang.

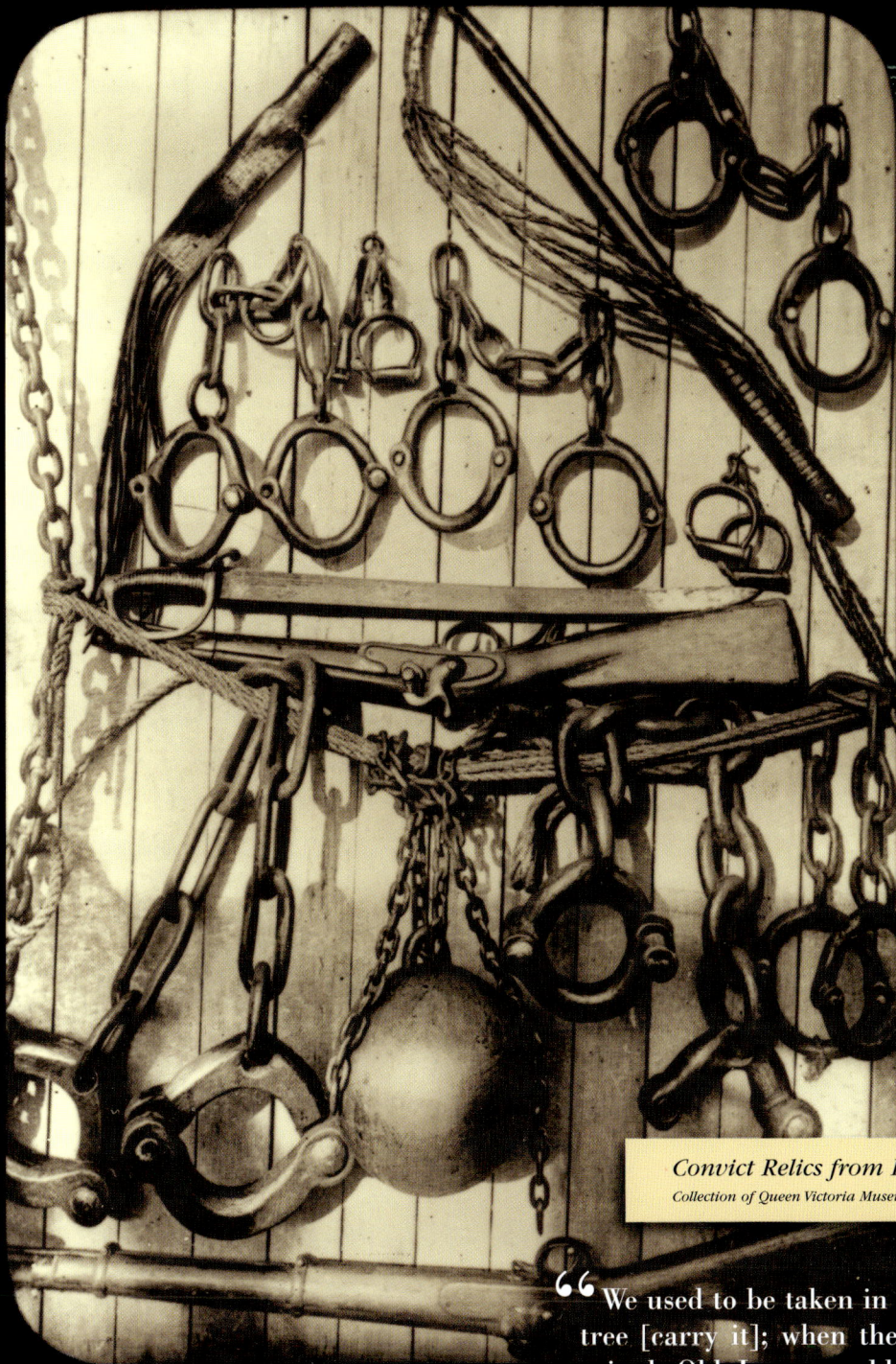

Convict Relics from Port Arthur, Tasmania
Collection of Queen Victoria Museum and Art Gallery, Launceston, Tasmania

"The way they floged them was theire arms pulle round a large tree and their breasts squezed against the tree so the men had no power to cringe or stir.

There were two flogers, Richard Rice and John Jonson, the Hangman from Sidney. Rice was a left handed man and Johnson was right handed so they stood at each side and I never saw two thrashers in a barn moove there stroakes more handeyer than those two killers did … tho' I was two perches from them, the flesh and skin blew in my face as they shooke of the cats."

— GENTLEMAN FARMER, JOSEPH HOLT, 1838.

"We used to be taken in large parties to raise a tree [carry it]; when the body of the tree was raised, Old Jones would call some of the men away — then more; the men were bent double — they could not bear it — they fell — the tree on one or two, killed on the spot.

Many a time I have been yoked like a bullock with twenty or thirty others to drag along timber. About eight hundred died in six months at a place called Constitution Hill.

I knew a man so weak, he was thrown into the grave, when he said, 'Don't cover me up. I'm not dead; for God's sake don't cover me up!' The overseer answered, 'Damn your eyes, you'll die tonight, and we shall have the trouble to come back again!'"

— JOSEPH SMITH, TRANSPORTED AGED 14,
IN A LETTER TO CAROLINE CHISHOLM, 1852.

A Chance to Escape

PRISONERS HEARD STORIES from their guards of Dutch and English settlements in Hong Kong, Singapore and Batavia (Indonesia). They really had no idea at all of where they were, and gave little thought to how they would get to these settlements, but believed that if they could live on native foods and animals for a few days, they could walk their way back to civilisation.

While most 'bolted' for the bush, some stole boats and made their way up the coast. Others simply ran away and joined indigenous tribes, or survived by attacking and stealing food from free settlers until they were eventually captured or killed. They were the first true 'bushrangers'.

There is no knowing how many perished in their desperate bid for freedom, but it was known that the Sydney bush was ringed with the bleached bones of those who never made it.

When a man at large grew weary of his isolation, was tired and hungry and living in constant fear, he could give himself up, accept his **mandatory** 50 lashes and go back to hard labour to serve out the rest of his sentence. Is it any wonder that so many preferred to stay out and die 'free'?

Flogging Prisoners, Tasmania
(drawing by James Reid, 185-?) Petherick Collection, National Library of Australia, an6332106

IN JANUARY 1792, the muster of convicts at the end of the day showed that 44 men and nine women were missing.

Most of them would have become hopelessly lost in the 'perfect maze that was made by nature that was the foothills of the Blue Mountains' and perished, only a few would have wandered back into the settlement, starving and exhausted.

This happened so often that one 'bolter' wrote: **'to deter all others who now do or shall in future, entertain any idea of regaining their liberty … nothing but inevitable death must be the final event … CHINA DOES NOT LAY BEYOND THE MOUNTAINS.'**

The Sad Story of Mary Bryant

MARY BRYANT and her husband William were transported aboard the convict ship *Charlotte*. Mary had been convicted of stealing, William had been caught smuggling – not an unusual crime along the Cornish coast where they lived.

Mary gave birth to a baby girl on the voyage out, who they named Charlotte after the ship.

William was one of the few convicts who had any useful skills and was put in charge of the colony's fishing fleet, but was caught selling some fish on the sly and was beaten, given 100 lashes for this seemingly small crime.

He decided to make a bid for his freedom. With seven other men, Mary and their two children, William stole the governor's own six-oared cutter and rowed silently away from the prison at night on 29 March 1791.

Once through the heads they were free and headed north towards New Guinea. Mary Bryant navigated the small craft safely all the way along the coast to Cape York where they turned west until they reached the Dutch settlement at Koepang in Timor on 5 June.

This was the first time that anyone had travelled up the east coast of Australia since Captain James Cook had made his journey of discovery 20 years earlier. Back then, Cook had rammed the *Endeavour* onto the coral reefs and lay stranded for several months until the ship could be repaired.

At Koepang, the escapees pretended they were survivors from a shipwreck and the Dutch governor took them in and offered his hospitality until they could join a ship headed for England.

For some unknown reason, William Bryant told the governor the true story of their voyage, and they were all immediately put behind bars. They were then transferred to Batavia (Indonesia). While awaiting the arrival of a British ship, the first tragedy struck; both William and his son Emmanuel died just before Christmas 1791.

Mary and Charlotte Bryant were taken into the custody of the British man-o-war the *Gorgon* which was returning to England with a marine detachment on board. Royal Marine Watkin Tench who had been on the *Charlotte* with the First Fleet remembered Mary Bryant and described both her and William as 'a decent pair, distinguished by their good behaviour'. But there was more sadness for Mary, her daughter Charlotte died on 7 May and was buried at sea.

When she arrived back in England, Mary Bryant was all alone. She faced imprisonment again and transportation back to Botany Bay.

Her heroic adventure was taken up by the renowned journalist James Boswell. She was pardoned in 1793 and retired into obscurity back in her native Cornwall. As a gesture of goodwill, Boswell gave Mary a pension providing her with £10 per year.

THE FIRST BUSHRANGERS

'Convicts' Letter Writing at Cockatoo Island N. S. W.
(Phillipe de Vigors, 1849) Mitchell Library, State Library of New South Wales

P.D.V. March 1st 1849. "Convicts" Letter writing at Cockatoo Island N.S.W. "Canary Birds"!

The 'Canaries' Take Flight

CONVICTS were given the nickname 'canary birds' because of the bright yellow colour of their prison 'slops' [clothing]. It would not have been difficult to spot these fellows in the street; no wonder they bolted for the bush!

However, there were a lot of convicts who were legitimately 'at large' while in the service of their masters. In the very earliest days of the settlement in Van Diemen's Land, when the supply ships failed to arrive the settlement was faced with starvation.

The authorities ordered the release of a number of prisoners, gave them arms and sent them into the bush to hunt kangaroos and other wild animals.

Even after the ships had arrived and the food shortage was over, a lot of these 'liberated' convicts were not keen to give up their freedom.

In September 1810, Governor Davey made the first reference to 'a gang of bushrangers' who had refused to come back into prison. These men were led by a bolter named John Whitehead who had been transported twice and no doubt this time preferred to stay out of gaol.

A **proclamation** issued on 14 May 1813 called on these 'bolters' to surrender; those who ignored the proclamation were thereafter 'outlawed'. Beyond that point, they had nothing to lose but their lives.

Portrait of a Convict (Unknown)
Allport Library and Museum of Fine Arts, State Library of Tasmania

'Black' Caesar

THE 'HONOUR' of being named Australia's first bushranger fell to runaway convict, pick-pocket and petty thief, West Indian John 'Black' Caesar.

Caesar had arrived on the First Fleet, but bolted for his freedom after only two years in the settlement. Punishment for his escape was death by hanging, although the governor decided against it as he had some sympathy for the former slave.

Caesar escaped again, and again avoided the noose when he shot and killed the Aborigine Pemulwuy, who had been terrorising the settlers, and for this the whole colony was grateful.

Caesar bolted again, but this time a reward of five gallons of rum was put on his head. While at large, he survived by hunting and fishing and was also helped out by people living in the bush, both free and convicted.

The governor was worried that other convicts and some sympathetic settlers may have been supplying Caesar with guns and powder, so he issued this warning:

'The governor thinks it necessary to inform those settlers or people employed in shooting … that if it shall be discovered that they have so abus'd the confidence placed in them as to supply those common plunderers with any part of their ammunition, steps will be taken immediately for their punishment, as they will be considered accomplices in the robberies committed by those whom they have so supplied.'

'Black' Caesar was shot and killed by a man named Winbow at Liberty Plains near Sydney on 15 February 1796.

John Whitehead

JOHN WHITEHEAD was one of those bolters who preferred to stay free rather than comply with Governor George Arthur's call for all convicts-at-large to surrender in May 1813. He gathered around him a band of 60 to 80 fellows also set on freedom from their chains.

Whitehead was flogged publicly in 1800 during his first term of imprisonment, and then had been transported to Van Diemen's Land for a second term of seven years for the seemingly petty crime of stealing two pairs of breeches in 1801.

These convict bushrangers in John Whitehead's gang were not at all like the 'gentlemen of the bush' who roamed the goldfields 50 years later; they were men who had been brutalised and were brutal to others in return.

When Whitehead heard that one of his men had turned police informant, he had a pair of moccasins made of bullock-hide, filled them with bull-ants and strapped them to the man's feet. He died in agony.

Whitehead was mortally wounded in a shootout with the law in October 1814. Just before he died, he begged his 'brother in arms', the vicious Michael Howe, to cut off his head so that his body could not be identified.

Howe apparently did as he was requested, as the following notice appeared in the *Hobart Town Gazette* in 1817: **'A human head has been found near New Norfolk wrapped up in a handkerchief … we may therefore presume it is the remains of the misled culprit [Whitehead].'**

Skirmish between Bushrangers and Constables, Illawarra
(watercolour by Augustus Earle, 1827) Rex Nan Kivell Collection NK12/49, National Library of Australia, an2818470

Michael Howe — The Worst of the Worst!

MICHAEL HOWE is credited with causing the attacks of **retribution** by natives against white settlers in Van Diemen's Land which left many dead on both sides of the conflict.

It began after Whitehead was killed and Howe took control of his gang. He attacked a native camp to steal for himself and his gang some 'wives' from the natives. Naturally enough, the natives resisted but Howe persisted and many were shot.

Many of the black women seemed happy enough to stay with the white men, and it is said that Howe's 'wife' Black Mary assisted him on most of his escapades, her knowledge of the bush allowed him to escape from many attempts at his capture.

He regarded himself as the 'Lieutenant-Governor of the Woods' and even attempted to explain to the Governor Hon. T. Davey that he had never committed murder and only used violence when it was necessary to avoid capture. Davey sent a reply to Howe stating that if they gave themselves up, no charges would be laid for 'their acts while in the bush'. Howe was able to move freely about in Hobart Town where he became quite a celebrity, but when he learned that Davey was not going to honour his promise, he headed back to the bush. Davey had Howe declared an outlaw and the price of £100 placed on his head. He was captured by two **ticket-of-leave** men who in the attempt to bring him in were both mortally wounded by Howe.

In October 1818, a kangaroo hunter named Warburton guided two troopers to where Howe was camped in dense bush on the Shannon River. Howe rushed into the bush where he slipped down an embankment allowing one trooper to catch up with him. Howe and Trooper Worrall stood facing each other, pistols at the ready. Howe shouted 'Black beard against grey beard for a million' and fired but missed. Worrall took his aim and struck, Howe staggered back and as he was about to steady himself, the other trooper 'Big Bill' Pugh rushed forward and bashed Howe's skull in with the butt of his rifle.

Howe's body was buried where he fell, and his severed head taken to Hobart where it was put on display as a lesson to anyone who thought they too may bolt for the bush.

Gypsey

'GYPSEY' GEORGE SHIRLEY was an unusual candidate for the role of bushranger. A free-born Englishman who had ventured to Van Diemen's Land of his own accord, he married soon after he had arrived in the colony. His wife died in childbirth so he took to the bush. He joined up with a band of high-spirited adventurers roaming the highways. Before long, 'Gypsey' George Shirley was declared an outlaw.

At times, his band ran with the Aboriginal bandits known as Musquito, Black Jack and Black Tom who were raiding the white settlers around Hobart, taking their revenge after Howe had treated their fellow natives so badly. The gang sometimes numbered over 100 men and they were such a menace that the settlers lived in fear for their lives.

One settler John Thornley wrote that he had seen Gypsey in battle. He described Gypsey as tall, broad-shouldered and muscular, as cool as a cucumber and oblivious to the shots fired about him. Thornley said that 'he was one of the finest men I ever saw'.

Gypsey was killed near New Norfolk by troopers who had come upon him while he was skinning a sheep. Thornley was passing by and recognised the dead man. Unopened letters were found on his body. His coat — hanging on a tree nearby — contained a purse filled with one pound notes. The trooper took these into his custody.

CONVICTS PLUNDERING SETTLERS' HOMESTEADS.

Governor Davey's Proclamation to the Aborigines, 1816 National Library of Australia Collection, an6428965

Musquito

MUSQUITO WAS A PORT JACKSON native who had been transported to Tasmania for the murder of an Aboriginal woman, possibly his wife, in 1823.

He worked as an Aboriginal tracker and was responsible for the capture of a large number of bushrangers. After Michael Howe was killed, Musquito was no longer required and was dismissed without reward. Angry and despised by fellow convicts, he took to the bush joining the Oyster Bay tribe who were also taking their revenge on the white man.

He was captured by another Aborigine named Tegg who had fired on him as he lay resting by his campfire. When the sentence of death was passed on him, Musquito answered: 'hanging no bloody good for blackfellow … very good for whitefellow, he used to it'.

He was hanged in Hobart in February 1825, alongside 'Black Jack' and 'Black Tom' from the Oyster Bay tribe, who had also ridden with Gypsey.

PORT ARTHUR

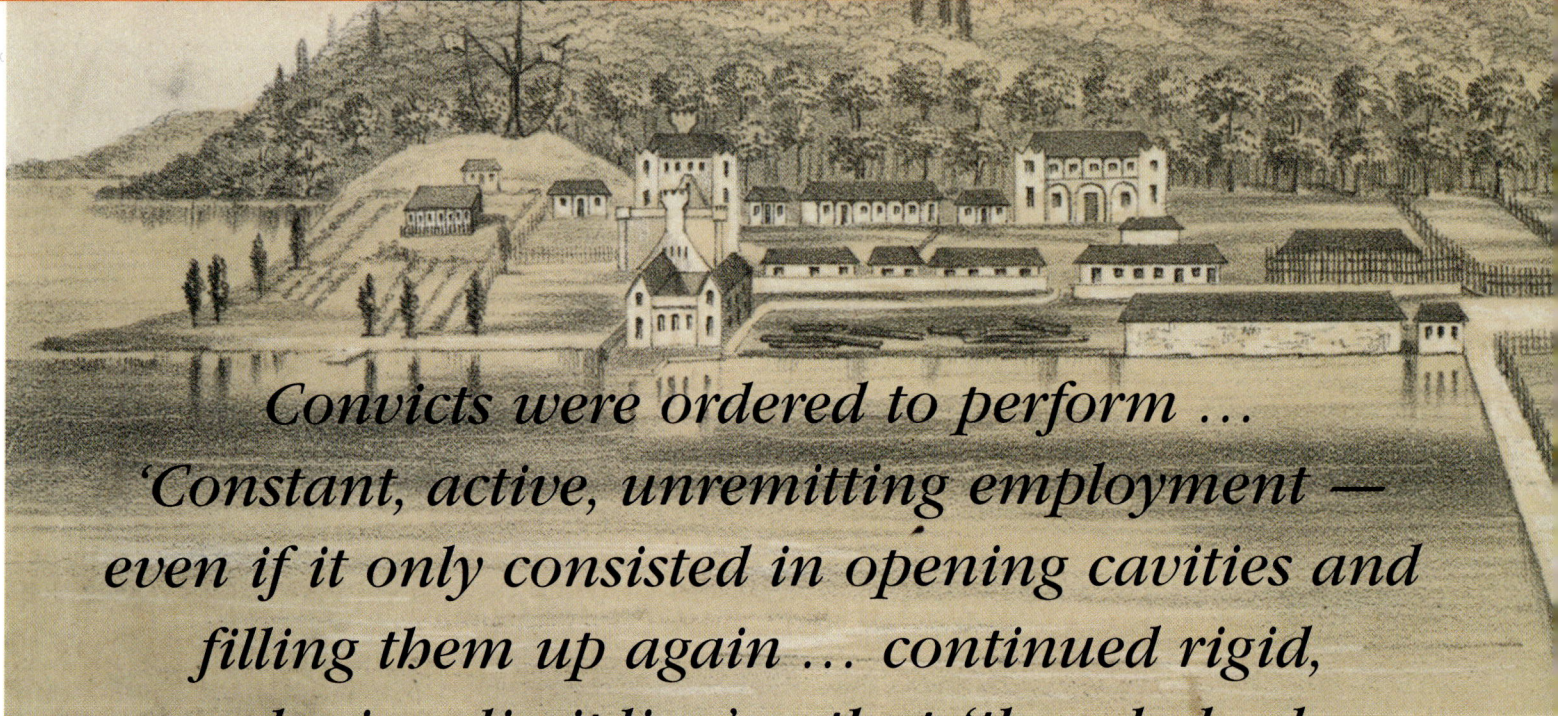

*Convicts were ordered to perform ...
'Constant, active, unremitting employment —
even if it only consisted in opening cavities and
filling them up again ... continued rigid,
unrelaxing discipline,' so that, 'the whole class
of Convicts would absolutely dread the very
idea of being sent there.' — GEORGE ARTHUR*

THE **penitentiary** at Port Arthur in Van Diemen's Land was a house of horrors resting on one of the prettiest harbours on the island. However, very few who ever lived there enjoyed the beauty of its setting. Port Arthur must have seemed to have been at the very bottom of the world, as far from old England as it was possible to go. There, the Queen's laws were rigorously upheld, and little care was given to those who could not survive the brutal force of her justice.

Not far away was Macquarie Harbour, another charming setting for the Crown to take its vengeance on the miscreant.

The men sent there were not men to be trusted, they were the habitual criminals, the repeat offenders, the murderous refuse of other prisons.

There was another place worse than this, even further away for the 'worst of the worst'. That place was a living hell in an endless ocean — a thousand miles from the mainland — its name was Norfolk Island.

Alexander Pearce, 'the Cannibal' Executed
Mitchell Library, State Library of New South Wales

The 'Cannibal' Pearce

AFTER THE DESTRUCTION of Howe and his gang, Lieutenant-Governor George Arthur wrote to the Colonial Secretary in 1822 proudly announcing that bushranging had been 'totally suppressed in Van Diemen's Land for the past three years'.

He had not reckoned on the likes of Alexander Pearce and eight other convicts who escaped from Macquarie Harbour on 20 September 1822.

They doused all the signal fires on the shore, stole a boat and headed away from the prison. Landing a little way up the coast, they smashed the boat to pieces and took to the bush. For eight days, they marched on until they were exhausted and very hungry.

One man, Bob Greenhill, said he was so hungry he could eat a piece of man, and that set the others to thinking. They agreed that it was to be one in, all in, and selected their first victim. Alexander Dalton was the first to die, his crime was that he had once been a **flogger**, and for that he deserved to die.

Over the next few days, the strongest dealt the weakest a mortal blow until, in the end, only Pearce and Greenhill were left alive, each having dined on the flesh of their fellow escapees. While Greenhill was sleeping, Pearce grabbed the axe from beneath him and struck a fatal blow. He cut off a thigh and one arm, travelling on for four more days until that too was eaten.

Pearce kept wandering through the bush until he came upon some sheep, so he killed a lamb and got stuck in. When the shepherd returned, he caught Pearce and threatened to report him to his master. Pearce threatened to shoot him instead.

Pearce joined up with Davis and Cheetham, a couple of bolters who marauded farms, stole sheep and generally made a real nuisance of themselves around Hobart Town.

Eventually they were caught but no one ever knew what had happened in the almost impenetrable bush. Pearce was only charged with sheep stealing and was sent back to Macquarie Harbour.

He escaped again, this time with a young man named Thomas Cox. Cox tasted little freedom. As soon as they had reached the other side of the harbour, Pearce had killed him and set to feasting on his flesh.

Lieutenant Cuthbertson thought Pearce's campfire was a distress signal, so he went across to investigate. He found Pearce dressed in Cox's clothes with little left of the poor boy save his bones and innards. Pearce had already scoffed the rest.

When he was taken before the court, his story horrified the good citizens of Hobart. Pearce said that he had developed a craving for human flesh, that 'it was delicious; far better than fish or pork'.

He was hanged before a huge crowd in Hobart Town on 5 August 1824.

The 'Monster' Jeffery

THOMAS, OR MARK, JEFFERY, JEFFRIES or Jefferies arrived in Van Diemen's Land aboard the brig *Harvies* on 22 April 1822.

He had been a useful prisoner, a flogger and executioner, and was rewarded for his efforts with employment as a watch-house guard, but he soon began to abuse this position of trust.

Jeffery had a weakness for strong drink and the grog was to ruin him. He was first caught drunk, then caught taking a female prisoner out of the watch-house. Although he was fined for these offences, he didn't stop there. He bolted and was flogged 50 lashes then sent to Macquarie Harbour for 12 months for threatening a constable with a knife.

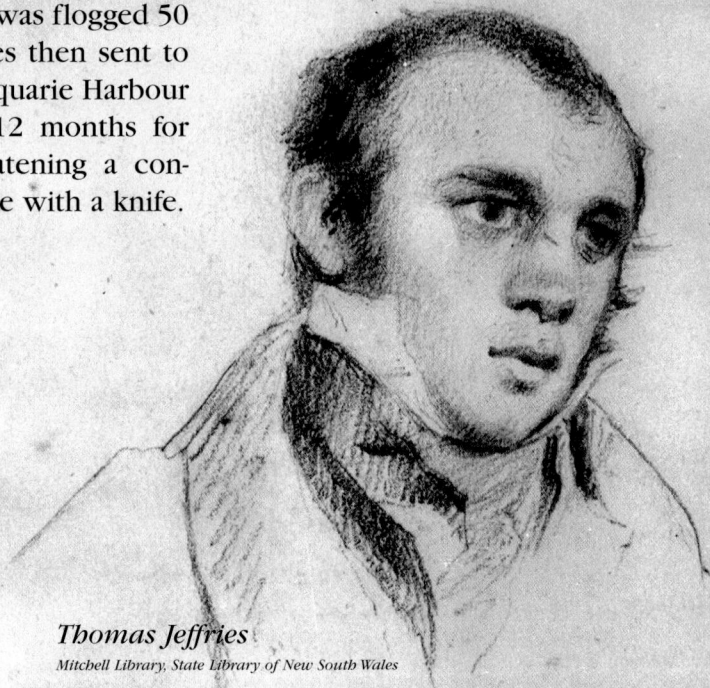

Thomas Jeffries
Mitchell Library, State Library of New South Wales

Jeffery escaped from Macquarie Harbour in 1825 with two other convicts, Hopkins and Russell. When their food ran out after a few days, they made a pact, and tossed a coin to see who would be sacrificed to save the others. Jeffery and Hopkins dined on Russell's flesh for the next five days until they came upon some sheep.

By now Jeffery was committed to the outlaw life, yet he seemed to have little regard for the lives of others.

When he held-up the homestead of Mr Tibbs, he committed the cruel act for which he was hanged. First he shot the stockman who refused to go into the bush with him, and forced Mr and Mrs Tibbs across an open paddock. Mrs Tibbs complained that she could not keep up the pace as she was carrying her five-month-old baby clutched to her breast.

Jeffery grabbed the infant and beat it against a tree, then asked Mrs Tibbs if she could go faster now. Mr Tibbs turned and rushed at him but Jeffery was too fast, he shot him, then simply walked away leaving Mrs Tibbs alone to mourn her dead.

It was the bounty hunter John Batman who tracked Jeffery down and brought him to justice. Batman had been engaged by the authorities to track and capture bushrangers, and was also responsible for the capture of Matthew Brady with whom Jeffery had ridden until he was kicked out of Brady's gang for molesting women.

Jeffery was the man that Brady despised most — a baby killer and callous murderer. It took a struggle with his gang to prevent Brady from attacking the Launceston lock-up, freeing the prisoners and hauling Jeffery from his condemned cell and flogging him to death.

When Jeffery was being delivered from Launceston to Hobart Prison, the public throng almost pulled him from the cart and would have **lynched** him on the spot if they had succeeded. Jeffery was convicted and sentenced to be hanged on 4 May 1826.

He stood on the gallows alongside the bushrangers Bryant, Perry, Thompson and Matthew Brady, who protested bitterly at having to be hanged alongside 'The Monster' Jeffery. Brady's protest fell on deaf ears, the trapdoor swung open and they dropped into eternity together.

South-west View of Macquarie Harbour
(drawing by Thomas Lempriere, c. 1827) Petherick Collection, National Library of Australia, an4921367

'It has caused Matthew Brady much concern that such a person known as George Arthur is at Large. Twenty gallons of rum will be given to any person that can deliver his person to me.'
— MATTHEW BRADY

The Brady Gang

MATTHEW BRADY WAS A CHARMING young man: able to read and write and he was also a good horseman. This good-looking young man had forged his master's signature to pay off a debt, and for this was sentenced to seven years transportation.

Brady didn't take at all well to prison life in Macquarie Harbour after he landed there aboard the *Julianna* in 1820. He was constantly in trouble — 25 lashes for neglect of duty, 25 more lashes for not going to the barracks with his work gang at the proper time, 50 more for going on board a ship planning to escape, 50 more for remaining absent for three days.

By the time he eventually did manage to escape, Brady had received a total of 350 lashes for his repeated attempts at freedom.

Along with 14 others, Brady managed to break free from Macquarie Harbour and arrived near Hobart Town on 9 June 1824.

With this gang of outlaws, Brady raided homesteads and farmhouses, plundering as they went.

The only thing that distinguished Brady's gang from other marauding gangs was the courtesy that he offered to any women that he came in contact with. While his men were allowed to steal whatever they wished, and to kill if necessary, they were instructed to treat women with respect and honour and never to injure a defenceless person.

Brady openly mocked the governor who seemed to have no luck at all in bringing him in. There were many settlers who relished the displeasure that the cheeky young bandit gave to George Arthur, but he was eventually betrayed by one of his own men who was pardoned and given a ticket back to England for his services.

The 'traitor' Cowan led the 40th Regiment to Brady's campsite. While several of the gang were killed in the bloody battle that followed, Brady escaped into the bush. He was tracked by John Batman and his team of Aboriginal trackers.

Brady and Batman stood face to face. Brady asked Batman if he was a military officer, when Batman replied that he was not, Brady gave himself up, saying that he would never have surrendered to a soldier.

Much to Brady's disgust, he was transported to Hobart in the same cart as Jeffery, and refused to sit on the same side as the baby killer. At Brady's trial, women wept openly for him and his condemned cell was filled with flowers, baskets of fruit and confectionery given by well-wishers to sweeten his darkest hour.

When his time to die had come, Brady was forced to stand on the gallows alongside Jeffery. In the end, 'he died more like a patient **martyr** than a felon murderer'.

Matthew Brady Mitchell Library, State Library of New South Wales

Macquarie Harbour

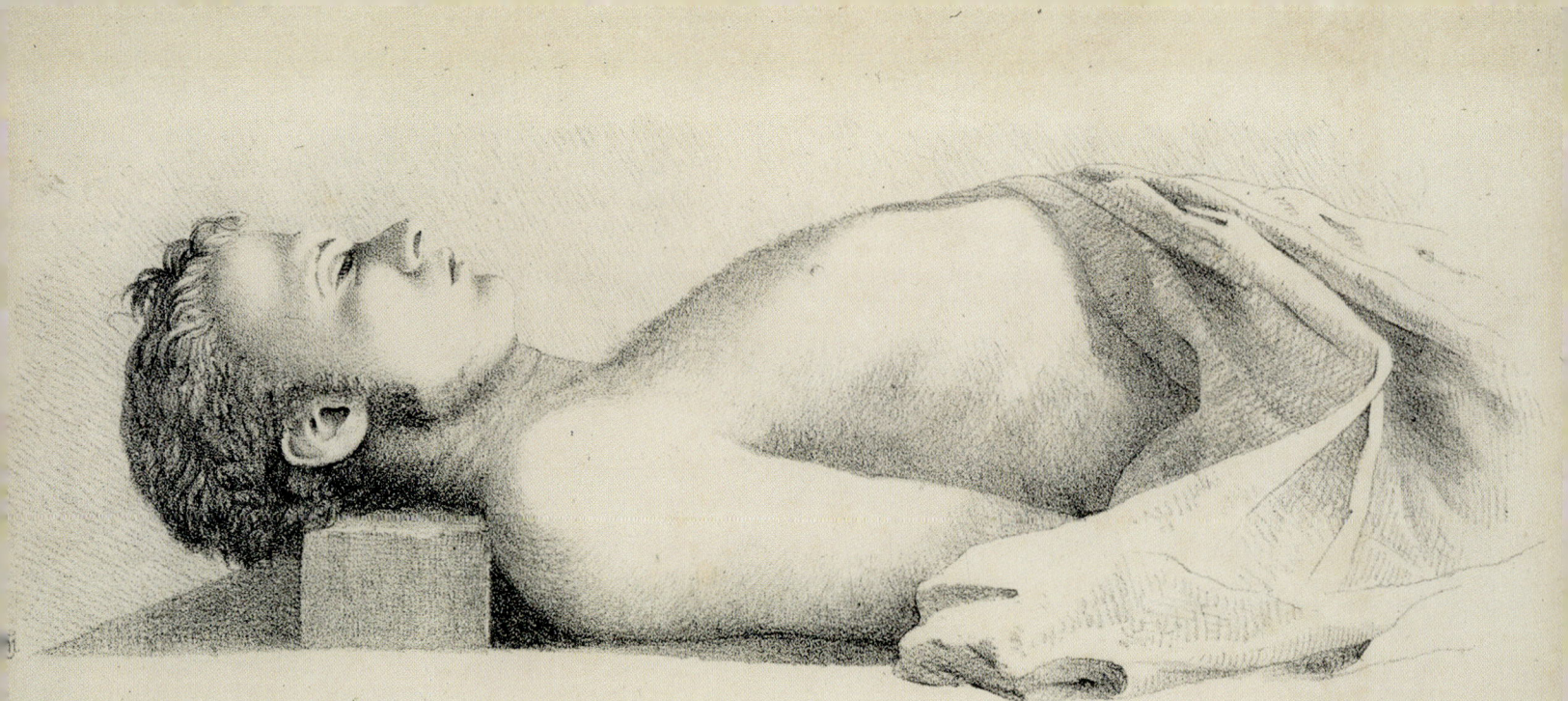

John Donohoe, c. 1830
(drawing by Thomas Mitchell)
Mitchell Library, State Library of New South Wales

DONOHOE.

The Last of the Convict Outlaws

'Bold' Jack Donohoe

JOHN DONOHOE was transported to Botany Bay arriving aboard the *Ann and Amelia* on 2 January 1825. He was assigned to a settler in Parramatta, but was in trouble almost as soon as he started. He spent some time on the chain gang but broke away and took up robbing wagons and **bullock-drays** on the Windsor Road.

This kind of robbing was easy: the wagons moved so slowly that Donohoe and his mates Kilroy and Smith didn't even need a horse. Before long, they were captured and sentenced to be hanged. Kilroy and Smith were hanged, but Donohoe managed to escape between the court and the cells.

He joined a gang of Irish and English bolters who ranged across the Liverpool, Parramatta and Windsor districts where they robbed in true 'Robin Hood' style. Taking from the well-to-do, the gang fenced their booty through the scores of poor settlers and 'ticket-of-leave' farmers who welcomed the opportunity to benefit from Donohoe's daring deeds.

They once robbed the farmhouse of the well-known explorer Charles Sturt. When Donohoe recognised Sturt, he apologised, directing his mates to 'stand back boys — we don't rob him'. However, when they robbed the less popular Reverend Samuel Marsden, they didn't spare him the same generosity.

Donohoe was eventually betrayed by one of his gang who may have responded to the reward of 'pardon and passage' offered by the governor. Jack Walmsley led the troopers to Donohoe's camp in the bush near Campbelltown to save his own neck. Donohoe, realising that this time there was no escape for him, waved his hat in the air then shouted, 'We're ready, if there's a dozen of you…', but he never finished his cry. Trooper John Muggleston had raised his pistol and shot 'Bold' Jack straight through the forehead.

Within days of his death in the bush, one enterprising shopkeeper in Sydney had produced a line of clay pipes with an **effigy** of 'Bold' Jack complete with the tiny bullet-hole in the forehead.

22

'Bold' Jack Donohoe — The Wild Colonial Boy

DUBLIN-BORN JOHN DONOHOE has the honour of having several ballads penned to commemorate his exploits on the roads of New South Wales, the most famous was 'The Wild Colonial Boy' which became Australia's first unofficial anthem.

The tune was based on the rebellious Irish ballad 'The Wearin' of the Green', and simply singing it could land the singer in gaol. The name of the song was changed from its original title 'Bold John Donohoe' to 'The Wild Colonial Boy', and 'Donohoe' to 'Doolan' to avoid the scrutiny of the authorities.

It is known that 'The Wild Colonial Boy' was sung heartily in the Glenrowan Hotel the night before bushranger Ned Kelly was taken in 1880.

There was a Wild Colonial Boy,
Jack Doolan was his name.
Of poor but honest parents
He was born in Castlemaine,
He was his father's only hope,
His mother's pride and joy
And dearly did his parents love
Their Wild Colonial Boy.

Chorus
So come away, me hearties,
We'll roam the mountains high,
Together we will plunder,
And together we will die.
We'll scour along the valleys,
And we'll gallop o'er the plains,
And scorn to live in slavery,
Bound down by iron chains.

At the age of sixteen years
He left his native home,
And to Australia's sunny shore
A bushranger did roam.
They put him in the iron gang
In the government employ,
But never an iron on earth could hold
The Wild Colonial Boy.

In sixty-one this daring youth
Commenced his wild career,
With a heart that knew no danger
And no foeman did he fear.
He stuck up the Beechworth mail coach,
And robbed Judge MacEvoy
Who, trembling cold, gave up his gold
To the Wild Colonial Boy.

One day as Jack was riding
The mountainside along,
A-listening to the little birds,
Their happy laughing song,
Three mounted troopers came along,
Kelly, Davis and Fitzroy,
With a warrant for the capture of
The Wild Colonial Boy.

'Surrender now! Jack Doolan,
For you see it's three to one;
Surrender in the Queen's own name,
You are a highwayman'.
Jack drew a pistol from his belt,
And waved it like a toy,
'I'll fight, but not surrender,' cried
The Wild Colonial Boy.

He fired at trooper Kelly,
And brought him to the ground,
And in return from Davis
Received a mortal wound,
All shattered through the jaws he lay
Still firing at Fitzroy,
And that's the way they captured him,
The Wild Colonial Boy.

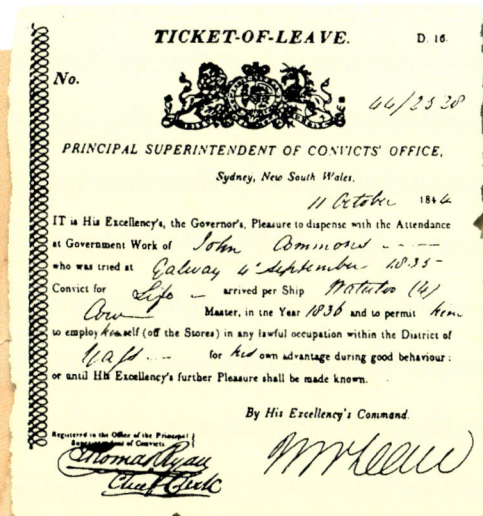

'Ticket-of-leave'

A 'ticket-of-leave' was granted to 'reformed' convicts who had done all or part of their time. The government was keen to get as many as possible off the government stores and 'ticket' convicts were expected to take up a bit of land and look after themselves in designated areas.

Few had any love for the troopers or their former gaolers and refused to hand over bushrangers, more often helping them stay clear of the law.

A Portrait of a Man in the Dock, Martin Cash
Allport Library and Museum of Fine Arts, State Library of Tasmania

The 'Brave but Unfortunate Irishman', MARTIN CASH

Martin Cash is the only famous Australian bushranger to have died peacefully in his own bed — aged sixty-seven [or sixty-eight].

MARTIN CASH was born in 1810 in the town of Enniscorthy, County Wexford, Ireland. His father had inherited his fortune and did his best to drink and gamble his life away. When he was only a teenager, Martin had also developed his father's fondness for the horse track, the gaming-room and the public bar.

By the time he was 16, Cash was running wild. One evening, after one of his companions told him that a rival suitor was seen visiting Cash's girlfriend, Martin marched to his girlfriend's house and shot his rival through the window.

Although the rival wasn't killed, Cash was arrested and sent for trial. He was sentenced to be transported for seven years.

He arrived in Botany Bay aboard the *Marquis of Huntley* in January 1828, aged 18 years.

Martin must have behaved himself as he did his time and was granted a ticket-of-leave. He settled down as a farm-hand in the Hunter Valley of New South Wales.

One day, Cash was helping a friend brand some cattle when he discovered they were stolen. Knowing that punishment for cattle-theft was banishment to Norfolk Island, he immediately packed up and left for Van Diemen's Land with his partner Bessie Clifford.

Once in Hobart, he worked as a labourer, but bad luck seemed to follow the ex-convict. He was twice falsely accused of theft, but on the second occasion he thrashed the arresting officer so badly that he was caught and sentenced to a further seven years imprisonment.

Cash made his escape after two days and rushed back to where he had left Bessie. He was caught again and had a further nine months added to his sentence, and twelve months on the road gang. Cash ran away again, rushed back to pick up Bessie, but the pair were recognised as they waited on the docks to board ship. Cash was brought before the presiding magistrate John Price, who said to him, 'You will not best me

Allport Library and Museum of Fine Arts, State Library of Tasmania

C. Hutchins Lithographer

NORTH VIEW OF EAGLE HAWK NECK,
WHICH JOINS TASMAN'S PENINSULAR TO THE MAIN LAND OF VAN DIEMAN'S LAND.

THERE IS, AT THIS PLACE, A CHAIN OF DOGS, WHICH ARE SO SAVAGE, THAT SHOULD ANY CONVICT ESCAPE FROM THE
PENAL SETTLEMENT OF PORT ARTHUR, IT IS IMPOSSIBLE FOR THEM TO PASS INTO THE COLONY.

Martin Cash
Allport Library and Museum of Fine Arts,
State Library of Tasmania

robberies and got into fights and brawls. They built a stronghold of logs at Mount Dromedary where Cash was joined by Bessie, but he discovered that the troopers were following her. He sent Bessie back to town to be away from danger, but she was arrested and gaoled in the hope to lure the gang out of the hills.

Martin Cash wrote to the governor and demanded that she be freed, or he would come down and give the governor 'a sound flogging'. After Martin heard rumours that Bessie was being a little too friendly with some other fellows, he went into town in search of her. The jealousy that had caused him to commit his first act of criminal stupidity brought him undone again. Cash was again recognised on the streets. In an attempt to get away, he shot and mortally wounded a police constable.

Cash was caught again and sentenced to hang, but was reprieved and transported to Norfolk Island. Even though he was under the ever-watchful eye of John Price, Martin became a model prisoner. After Price left for Victoria, Cash was made a special constable and granted his ticket-of-leave.

He married Mary Bennet, the daughter of the island's medical officer, and they moved back to Van Diemen's Land where they had one son also named Martin.

After his son died of rheumatic fever in 1871, Martin was heartbroken and descended into alcoholism. He collapsed at the bar of the Lord Rodney Hotel and died on 26 August 1878 in his own bed in the farmhouse he had built for himself at Glenorchy in Tasmania.

Martin Cash lays buried in the Cornellian Bay Cemetery. His headstone bears the inscription: 'to the Memory of that brave but unfortunate Irishman MARTIN CASH'.

Martin Cash,' as he added a further two years to his existing sentence. Then, for good measure, Price gave him a new sentence of four more years in Port Arthur.

It was from Port Arthur that he made his most daring escape, braving the water and the dogs of Eaglehawk Neck along with fellow convicts Lawrence Kavanagh and George Jones. They had taken off their clothes and boots to carry them over their heads while they were in the water, but they were washed away. When the trio reached the other side, they scrambled ashore stark naked.

They held-up a hut-keeper, tied him to a post and stole his clothes. The following day they declared that they would take up arms and become outlaws — which is what they now were anyway!

The men became just like all the other gangs roaming the bush of Van Diemen's Land; they held-up travellers, attacked settlers, committed

CASH & Co. — The small gang of Martin Cash, Lawrence Kavanagh and George Jones were outlawed and a reward of £50 was placed on each of them. If any convict was able to lead the police to their whereabouts, he would also be granted a conditional pardon.

But no one ever gave them up. There were so many who had been treated so badly by the prison system, once granted their leave they were never going to dob on any other prisoner who was making their own desperate bid for freedom.

Lawrence Kavanagh

LAWRENCE KAVANAGH was a hard man from Waterford, County Wicklow, Ireland. He had been transported for life after he was convicted of the robbery of a house in Dublin on 24 August 1828.

Kavanagh had injured himself severely when he accidentally shot himself in the arm. The musket-ball entered his arm at the elbow, ran along the bone and came out at his wrist, leaving the arm totally useless. After several days of agony, he gave himself up to the authorities.

He was sent to the notoriously tough Norfolk Island prison. Even though there was no chance at all to escape from the island, Kavanagh did make an attempt to escape and received 150 lashes for his effort.

He was hanged along with 12 others, at the insistence of John Price after the bloody and murderous attacks on the prison guards by William 'Jacky Jacky' Westwood on 2 July 1846 in what became known as the 'Billy-can' mutiny.

Just before he was hanged, Kavanagh passed by Martin Cash, who was in charge of the tools used by stonemasons building a blacksmith's shop. Cash had taken no part in the riot. Kavanagh sneered at him: 'Martin, they have got you,' implying that his old mate was finally in the hands of the oppressors.

This accusation really cut Martin Cash to the core: he was just keeping himself out of trouble, he had suffered enough.

George Jones

GEORGE JONES was a Londoner who was transported to Botany Bay in 1830 for highway robbery.

He was the only one of Cash & Co. that escaped capture, and he continued to raid farms and houses, operating out of Cash's old hideout on the Mount. He teamed up with escaped convicts John Liddell and James Dalton who once held-up a hawker and left him tied to a tree after they had stolen everything they wanted from his cart.

The police laid a trap for them, capturing the men inside a hut they used sometimes on the Dromedary. One was shot as he tried to crawl away on his hands and knees, Jones was blinded by a faceful of buckshot as he rushed outside.

Both Liddell and Dalton were sentenced to death. The judge said that he could not consider any mercy for the bushrangers, to which Liddell replied: 'I don't want mercy from you or anyone else. I've been 11 years at Port Arthur and I don't want to go there again, I'd rather die than live.'

Seeming not to care what was about to happen, Dalton answered back: 'I don't care what you do.'

NORFOLK ISLAND

The 'Billy-can' Mutiny

NORFOLK ISLAND was the toughest prison of them all, few ever made it away from this tiny island hell. It was the place where the worst of the worst were sent, where no man was safe amongst his fellow criminal inmates, where no one had anything else left to lose — except their lives, and few even cared for that.

Every prisoner on the island had their own billy-can made as an item of barter by the mechanics in the prison. They took pride in this only possession that wasn't government issue, and generally left them on the mess tables when they went to bed.

On the night of 1 July 1846, the constables confiscated these 'unauthorised vessels' and locked them away. The next morning, some prisoners broke open the stores and took their cans back.

Among these men were Lawrence Kavanagh, Martin Cash's accomplice from Van Diemen's Land, and William 'Jacky Jacky' Westwood who had been convicted after a short bushranging career in New South Wales. Westwood was heard that day to bellow: 'I'm going to the gallows: I'll bear this oppression no longer,' and then he attacked. He burst into the cookhouse and killed the overseer with a single stroke of his cudgel. Dashing through a covered archway, he bashed a guard's brains out against a brick wall as he sat at his post. With about 20 other men, they attacked the guards at the nearby lime-kilns. Westwood had picked up an axe on the way and burst into the guards' quarters, killing two men in their beds.

1600 of the 1800 prisoners on Norfolk took their revenge that day on the men who had made their lives such a misery. The riot was stopped when troopers from the garrison fitted their bayonets to the rifles and prepared a frontal attack.

Ten of these men, including 'Jacky Jacky' Westwood and Lawrence Kavanagh, were hanged on 13 October for their part in the 'Billy-can' mutiny. Just as Westwood was about to meet his end, he proclaimed: 'I welcome death as a friend; the world, or what I have seen of it, has no allurements for me ... Out of the bitter cup of misery I have drunk from my sixteenth year — ten long years — and the sweetest draught is that which takes away from the misery of living death.'

Their lifeless bodies were tossed into a pit outside the cemetery known as 'Murderer's Mound'. John Price would not allow them to lie in consecrated ground.

Murderer's Mound Burial Ground, Norfolk Island

Collection of Queen Victoria Museum and Art Gallery Collection, Launceston, Tasmania

The Penal Settlement at Norfolk Island

La Trobe Library Collection, State Library of Victoria

A VIEW of QUEENBOROUGH on Norfolk-Island

John Price,
'The Monster of Norfolk Island'

JOHN PRICE was Civil Commandant of Norfolk Island from 1846 to 1853.

He had been Muster Master of Van Diemen's Land before this appointment and had carried out his duties there with 'exceptional rigour and cruelty'.

It was in Van Diemen's Land that Price first came into contact with Martin Cash and had punished him harshly.

At Norfolk Island, Price continued to brutalise the men under his charge until he was finally appointed as Inspector-General of Convicts in Victoria in 1854.

While the men on Norfolk Island were not sorry to see him go, many of the settlers in goldrush Victoria were not pleased to see him arrive there either.

Price was eventually murdered by a group of convicts from the hulk *Success* who were breaking rocks at the Gellibrand Quarries.

As Price walked among them, they complained of the harshness of their treatment, lack of

Norfolk Island was originally settled by the British because of the long straight pine trees found in abundance there.

The British Admiralty was fearful of losing access to supplies of timbers for ship-building from the Baltic, and sought to find a ready replacement.

Unfortunately, Norfolk pines are short fibred, prone to splintering and will snap without warning when put under pressure.

This made them totally unsuitable for the long spars needed for shipping.

So the ever-resourceful British turned the beautiful island into a prison instead.

adequate food and the degrading condition of the prison ships.

Price told them to make their complaints 'in the proper form'.

Avoiding further bureaucratic delay, one prisoner belted Price over the head with a shovel, the rest picked up rocks and stoned him to death.

There were few, even outside the prison system, who mourned Price's passing.

An End to Transportation

Scrubbing at the Convict Stain

IT WAS AROUND THE TIME of the death of 'The Wild Colonial Boy' that the free settlers began to lobby the British parliament seeking an end to the system of transportation.

The settlers were concerned that with the seemingly endless supply of convicts dumped on Australia's shores, they would never see the society develop into one freed of the convict stain.

Free men of influence were also beginning to discuss the possibility of joining all of the separate colonies into one federated nation, but these ideas were abhorrent to the British Government. After all, Australia had been a very useful dumping ground for its unwanted nuisances; what need was there for the inhabitants to be allowed to take care of their own destiny?

But this did not stop the 'Australians' from continuing with their demands.

The Anti-transportation League was formed at a conference held in Melbourne in 1851. It was announced in London in December 1853 that transportation to the Australian colonies was to cease.

Of course, the mass-migration to the goldfields had changed the need for transportation of convict labour as hundreds of thousands were making their way around the globe of their own free will.

The Last Ships

The *St Vincent* was the last convict ship arriving in Van Diemen's Land on 26 May 1853. However, transportation continued for another 15 years to the colony of Western Australia who needed a lot of help to establish a viable community at the mouth of the Swan River.

The convict ship the *Hougoumont* was the last to arrive in Fremantle when it discharged its human cargo of 229 convicts, including the Irish revolutionary John Boyle O'Reilly and 62 other Irish, on 10 January 1868.

A Degraded Society

The Anti-transportation League warned the British Government that unless the policy of transportation ceased, British settlers would quit the colonies. They advised that if their young people could not travel without feeling that they: 'were born in a degraded section of the globe, we are at a loss to imagine what advantages conferred by sovereignty of Britain can compensate for the stigma of the brand.'

Women Shipped In!

After 80 years of transportation, Britain had shipped to Australia's sunny shores 160,500 of its unwanted citizens of whom 24,700 were women.

It was not long before the Catholic wife of an Indian Army Captain, Mrs Caroline Chisholm, was filling ships in England with young women ready to address this obvious imbalance.

Port Arthur Shuts Down

An End to Horror

AFTER THREE-QUARTERS OF A CENTURY of suffering and degradation, the penal settlement at Port Arthur closed on 17 September 1877.

Although the last convict ship had arrived in 1853, it took more than twenty years for the remaining prisoners to serve out their terms and be free to leave. Many of those imprisoned were serving time for crimes committed in Australia.

The novelist Marcus Clarke visited the prison just a few years before it was closed, when it still housed 300 convicts, 13 convict invalids, eight convict lunatics, 166 paupers and 86 lunatics who were not convicts.

Clarke — who published Australia's first novel *For The Term of His Natural Life* in 1874 — was able to observe first hand what he had imagined in his monumental work that laid bare the horrors and desperation of the convicted:

'I saw Port Arthur for the first time before a leaden and sullen sky; and ... I felt there was a grim propriety in the melancholy of nature ...

For half a century the law has allowed the vagabonds and criminals of England to be subjected to a lingering torment; futile for good and horribly powerful for evil; and it is with feelings of the most profound delight that we view the probable abolition of the last memorial fraught with so much misery.'

Today Port Arthur is in ruins, few of its buildings remain intact; the guard tower and gates (below) remain as silent witness to the brutality of the past.

(background)
Settlement, Port Arthur
National Library of Australia Collection, an2479035R4442

(inset)
Port Arthur from the Commandant's Gate
Spurling Collection, National Library of Australia, an21697618-415

31

Glossary

British Crown — concept of ownership of, and allegiance to, the state that extends beyond politics.

bullock-drays — large wooden carts pulled by teams of bullocks. Although capable of carrying very large loads, their progress along the roads was excruciatingly slow.

colonies — territories over which a foreign power assumes control. These colonies are governed as if they are part of the 'mother country'.

convicts — people who have been found guilty of crime against society. Among those transported to Australia, many were also 'convicted' for political reasons.

effigy — a model, caricature or likeness of a public figure.

executioner — person whose job it is to carry out a sentence of death on another person, by order of the state or court.

flogger — a convict given the task of whipping his fellow convicts for bad behaviour, usually with a 'cat-of-nine-tails', a whip which has nine strands, often knotted along the strands.

flotilla — a small fleet of ships.

gibbet posts — a type of wooden cross on which executed prisoners were displayed. Their bodies were left to be picked at by crows, until their skeletons simply fell apart.

governor — an unelected person who is granted command over a colonised territory, usually of military rank.

infrastructure — built assets of the state — hospitals, roads, public buildings, etc.

lynched — act of execution without sanction of legal process, usually conducted by an angry mob.

mandatory — a compulsory act, applied without question.

martyr — someone who gives up themselves in support of their beliefs, often in defiance of the prevailing law.

penitentiary — a place of detention operated by the state.

proclamation — public order or command given by government.

retribution — revenge.

ticket-of-leave — once a convict had served part of a service, or proved to be no longer any threat to the community, they were granted a 'ticket' which allowed them to live within specified areas, on land they settled and provided for themselves. They were not permitted to leave the colony, or even the district to which they were assigned. Few took much notice of these rules, especially once gold had been discovered in New South Wales and Victoria.

Index

Waverton Press
Level 1
100 Bay Road
Waverton NSW 2060
Australia
Email: publishing@fivemile.com.au

First published 2004
All rights reserved
© The Five Mile Press

Designed by Geoff Hocking

Printed in China

National Library of Australia Cataloguing-in-Publication data:
Hocking, Geoff.
Bound for Botany Bay.
Includes index
For lower to middle secondary students.

ISBN 1 74124 092 1.

1. Convicts - Australia - History - Juvenile literature. I. Title. (Series: Australia in History).

994.02